AN EASY-READ COMMUNITY BOOK

WHAT WILL WE BUY?

BY CAROLINE ARNOLD

PHOTOGRAPHS BY GINGER GILES

Franklin Watts
New York/London/Toronto/Sydney
1983

Special thanks are due the following individuals and organizations whose cooperation made the photographs possible:

Margie Hanrahan; Rafael Hernandez; Frank Sloan; Davis IGA, Kent, Conn.; Judie Mills; Theresa Murphy; Vicki Fischman; Cathy Abate; Lydia Stein; Bea Stuart; The Ware House, Kent, Conn.; Kent Greenhouse; Jackie Memoli; Kurz Gulf Station, Kent, Conn; House of Books, Kent, Conn.; Polks Hobby Store; Grace and Vin Sainz, Sport Scene, Kent, Conn.; Skip Irving, Kent Beauty Salon.

A very special thanks to Country Clothes, Kent, Conn.

R.L. 2.5 Spache Revised Formula

Library of Congress Cataloging in Publication Data

Arnold, Caroline.
What will we buy?

(An Easy-read community book)
Summary: Briefly surveys types of goods and services available from a variety of stores and discusses how shoppers pay for their purchases.
1. Shopping—Juvenile literature.
[1. Shopping] I. Title. II. Series.
TX335.A76 1983   381'.1   82-17555
ISBN 0-531-04508-0

Text copyright © 1983 by Caroline Arnold
Illustrations copyright © 1983 by Franklin Watts, Inc.
All rights reserved
Printed in the United States of America
6 5 4 3 2 1

CONTENTS

Where Do People Shop?	5
What Kind of Store Will You Go To?	8
What Will You Buy?	14
How Will You Pay For It?	30

Where Do People Shop?

A long time ago there were no cities or towns. There were no factories or stores. People grew their own food, made their own clothes, and built their own houses.

Today most people do not do these things. Instead they work at jobs to earn money. Then they use the money to buy the things they need.

We can buy some of the things we need in our own neighborhoods. Some stores may be so close that we can walk there. What kinds of stores are in your neighborhood?

   Sometimes we cannot find
everything we need close by. In many
cities and towns most of the stores are
in the center of town. We may go there
in a car or by bus or subway. Some stores
are in tall buildings. Then we can ride an
elevator or an escalator to each floor.

Sometimes we go to shopping centers to buy things. Many stores are built together in a shopping center. Some shopping centers even have a roof over a center open place. The air inside is warm in winter and cool in summer. You can shop easily even when it is raining or snowing.

What Kind of Store Will You Go To?

Sometimes a store sells only one kind of thing. It may sell just meat, fruit, candy, or baked goods. Or it may sell just shoes, flowers, or sporting goods.

But it is not always easy to go to a different store for each thing you need to buy. Instead, you can go to a supermarket or department store.

A supermarket has all kinds of foods. Each kind of food is kept in its own place. You can find meats, milk, fruits, vegetables, and canned or frozen foods in a supermarket. You can also find things like soap and napkins.

You can put everything you want to buy into a big basket on wheels. Then you can pay for all of it at the checkout counter.

A department store sells all kinds of clothes and household goods. Each part of the store has just one kind of thing. There are departments for girls' clothes, boys' clothes, shoes, jewelry, records, toys, books, cookware, and many other things. A clerk can help you find what you need.

If you live in the country there may not be any stores nearby. Even in a city the stores near you may not have what you want. Then you can order what you need from a catalog.

A catalog is a big book. It has pictures of all the things that a store sells. It also tells how much they cost. You can ask the store to send you what you want. It will come to your house by mail.

Most stores sell things that are new. But sometimes old things are still good. Very old things are called antiques. Some people like to buy antiques.

Sometimes people sell things that they no longer need. You can often find good things to buy at second-hand stores, garage sales, or auctions.

Sometimes you can buy things from salespeople who come to your house. Maybe you have gone to houses in your neighborhood to sell things for your school or for your scout troop.

What Will You Buy?

People go shopping for many things. Everyone buys food.

We buy some food when it is fresh. Milk, fruits, vegetables, and meat taste best when they are fresh. We buy some foods that have been frozen. Ice cream, juices, and some desserts are in the frozen food department. Some foods also come in cans or boxes.

It is fun to choose good foods to eat.

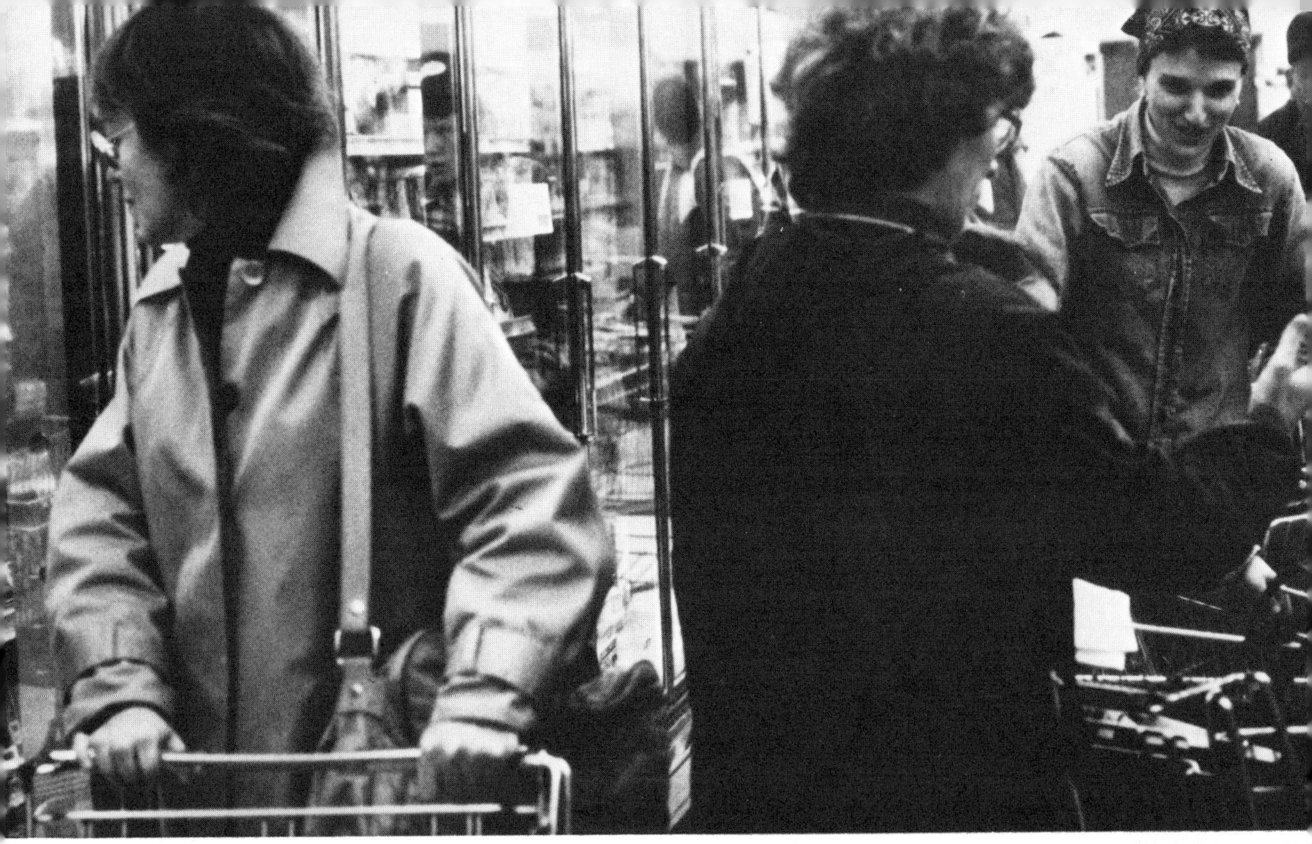

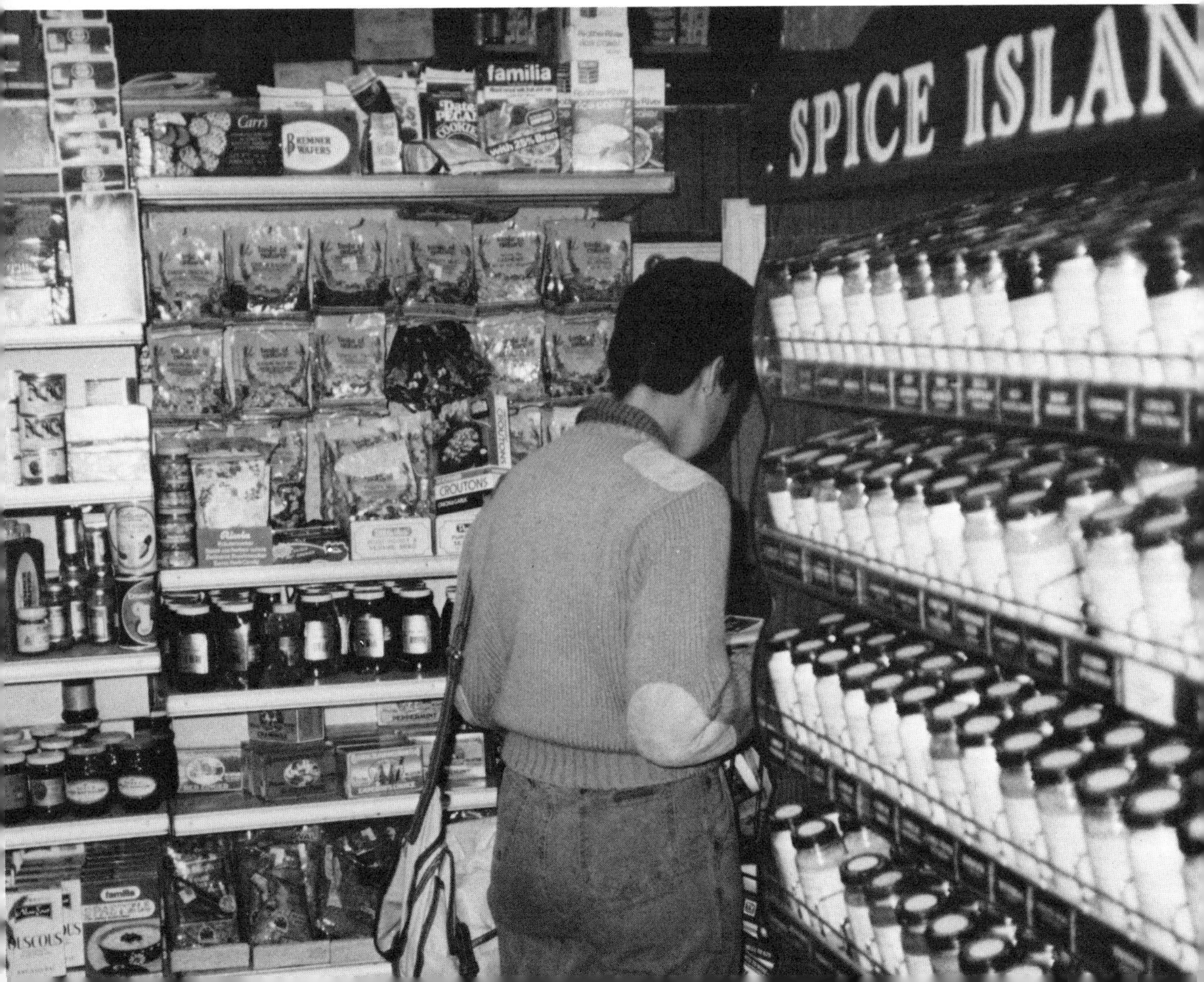
SPICE ISLAN
familia
Carr's
CROUTONS

Everyone buys clothes. Clothes help keep us warm in winter, cool in summer, and dry when it is raining.

People buy clothes when their old clothes wear out. Sometimes they buy clothes because they want to have a new style. And they buy clothes when their old ones no longer fit. Have you grown out of the clothes you wore last year?

You can buy clothes in many kinds of stores. Sometimes you have to try them on to see if they fit. It is fun to choose your favorite color and style of clothes.

Everyone needs a place to live.
Some people go shopping to buy their houses. A real estate company sells houses and land to people.
Some people rent a place to live. They pay money each month to the owner of the house or apartment.

We need to buy things to use inside the places we live. We buy rugs and furniture. We buy pictures and decorations to make our homes look nice. We buy dishes and kitchen supplies. We also buy things to keep our houses clean.

People who have yards and gardens need to buy yard equipment. They need lawn mowers, hoses, clippers, and many other things. They may also go to a garden store to buy seeds and plants.

Sometimes we want to build something. Or we may need to fix something. Then we may go to a hardware store or to a lumber yard to buy what we need. We go to a paint store when our house needs painting.

We all need to go to places in our communities. You may have a bike or roller skates to go to places in your neighborhood.

Many people buy cars and trucks to go places. People who have cars and trucks also need to buy gasoline and oil to make them work.

People also buy things to read. We buy books. We buy magazines and newspapers to find out the news.

We read to learn things. And we read for fun. We can buy things to read in a bookstore, at a newsstand, in a supermarket, and by mail.

We buy things for fun, too. Toy stores are full of many kinds of games and toys. Hobby stores have hobby supplies. Some people collect things like stamps, coins, or models. They can buy things at special stores, too. Do you have a hobby or a collection?

Sporting goods stores have things for people who like sports or camping. Sports like baseball, football, soccer, basketball, swimming, golf, and tennis need special clothes and equipment. What kind of sports do you like best?

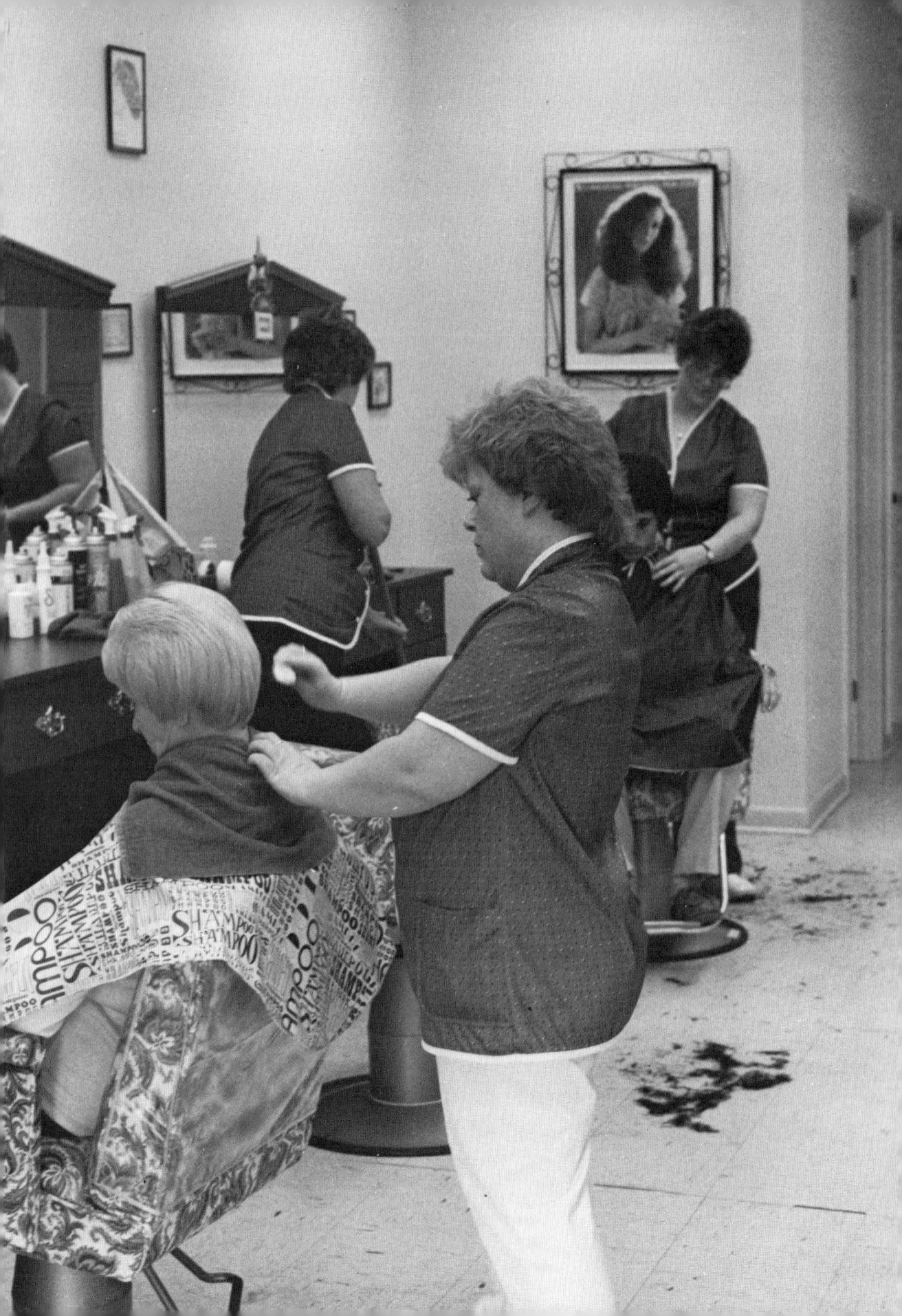

Some stores do not sell anything you can take home. Instead, you pay them to do something for you.

    A shoemaker fixes your shoes.

    A hairdresser cuts your hair.

    A travel agent helps to plan your vacation.

    You are buying these people's services when you go to their stores.

In every store there are many things to choose from. How can you decide what to buy?

For instance, if you are buying food, you will choose something you like to eat. You will also want to buy the right amount to feed your family.

You must also be sure that you have enough money to pay for what you want.

Some things cost more than others. Some things that cost more are bigger or better in some way. But sometimes you can find good things for less money. Stores sometimes have sales. They lower the prices of some things. Sometimes stores have discounts. Then they lower the prices of everything a little bit.

How Will You Pay for It?

Everything you buy costs money. You can pay your money in different ways.

Sometimes you pay cash. Then you pay with coins and bills. The clerk puts your money into a cash register. If you give more money than the item costs, you will get change. The cash register will also make a receipt for you. The receipt is a piece of paper that tells how much you paid.

Some people do not buy things with cash. They put their money in the bank. Then they buy things with checks. The store then takes the check to the bank to get the money.

Some people buy things with credit cards. When a person pays with a credit card the store gets its money from the credit card company. Then the person pays the same amount of money back to the credit card company.

There are many things to buy in your community. Some of them cost a lot of money. Some cost a little. You have to choose what to buy carefully. Then you will spend your money wisely.